PAT INGOLDSBY

IF YOU DON'T TELL ANYBODY I WON'T

WILLOW
PUBLICATIONS

First Published in 1996
by Willow Publications (Dublin),
3 Vernon Court,
Seafield Road West,
Clontarf, Dublin 3,
EIRE.

Cover Artwork/Phenomenal Help/
I'd Be Lost Without You: Steve Averill
Photographs for front and back cover/
You are uniquely talented: Almha Roche
Translation from the original
ogham carvings: Willow
Underwater photography,
spiritual direction and fleas: Hoot
Transport: My left and right legs
Distribution: My blue sack

ISBN: 0-9523052-24
Printed in Ireland by Colour Books Ltd.

WHERE?

Where could you write to me?
I slept in a doorway.

The door had a number on it.
Six . . I think.
It was cold.
Where could you write to me?

Where could you ring me?
I slept in a burnt-out car.
The number-plate was gone.
It was cold.

Where could you ring me?
Or write to me?
Or anything?

THE BIT YOU NEVER SEE

When the pub
is closed
and everybody
has gone home
the barman
opens up
the back
of the television
and removes
all the bodies.

FANCY FLYING ALL OVER THE PLACE

The woman on the train
pulled her jumper over her head
and said – "I'm not coming out."

The bicycle knelt forward
and prayed
because its front wheel
was gone.

The abandoned lorry
rusted to death
in the middle of a field
and awaited the Resurrection.

The woman scratched her neck
and her foot fell off.

The horse stood on top
of an empty hill
and took the full weight
of the sky on its back.

The priest said "Take this
and eat it"
but because his congregation
were really hungry
they ate him instead.

The sheep and lambs
fled across the field
without realising
that the train was running
away from them.

The little guy stuck his finger
into an empty 7-UP tin
and someone bit it off.

The flight of seagulls rose up
from a startled field
and a flight of cows
went straight up after them.

The driver announced
"Will persons not travelling
please leave the train"
and everybody got off.
"Fuck this" he said.
"I'm going home."
And he did.
Then everybody got on
again.

And so it goes.

VIOLATION

Sometimes news reports
say that a woman
has been
violently raped.
I think that rape
is always violent
even if you wear gloves
and whisper while
you're doing it.

FROM THE MOUTHS OF MACHINES

There are no conductors
on the buses anymore.
We don't need them.
We put our tickets
into a machine
instead.
We are becoming
cleverer
and cleverer.

There is nobody
in the signal-box
anymore.
We don't need them.
The level-crossing
opens and closes
all by itself.
We are becoming
ingenious.
We are becoming
so ingenious
that soon
there will be
nothing left
for us to do.

Then we will go
one stage further
and invent
a machine
which will do
the nothing for us.

One fine day
when nobody
is looking
the machines

will invent a man
who travels on the bus
and collects the tickets.
They will call him
a conductor.
They will invent
people who stand
behind counters
and dispense cash.
They will call them
bank officials.
They will invent
so many people
to do so many things
that there will be
nothing left
for them to do.

They will not invent people
to do the nothing for them.
They will all go off
to the beach instead
and build lovely sand-castles.

Exactly what we
should have done.

YOU TELL ME

The guy who
I see
when I look
into the mirror
looks out
and wonders
why I do
everything
that he
does.

LAST SUPPER

The man with nowhere to go
stood under
the cold petrified
night-time tree
in the middle of
O'Connell Street.
Because he had nothing
else to do
he joined up
all the white dots
which the birds
had dropped
onto the pavement
and he created
a perfect picture
of The Last Supper.
He wandered into it
and ate the bread
and drank the wine
and fell asleep
on the pavement
deep frozen
into the shape
of a cross.

PART OF THE REASON WHY LORD LIVINGSTON COTCHINEAL LEFT HIS WIFE AND WENT TO LIVE IN AN ENCLOSED ORDER

Lady Ebenezer Cotchineal
leaned forward
in the restaurant
and the shadows
from the feathers
on her hat
merged
with the shadows
of the electric fan
to form
a perfect windmill
on the wall.
Just then
Don Quixote
cantered in
from the street
in search
of something new
and exciting
to tilt.
Don
and his donkey
thundered towards the wall
with such ferocity
that nobody
who heard it
will ever forget
the thud.

"Let that be a lesson
to you"
said Lady Ebenezer.
"All my sympathies
are with your donkey."

Then she went home
and stuck
bigger feathers
in her hat.

I'LL TELL YOU WHAT SORT OF A DAY TODAY IS

On a day like this
if there is only
one wet seat
in the entire
Dublin Bus fleet
I am sure
to sit
on it.

HE THOUGHT THEY'D BE THRILLED TO
HEAR IT HE REALLY DID

The lift was full of people.
The lift was full of silence.
The lift was full of people
who would have loved
to say something
if only they could think
of something to say.
The man spoke suddenly.
The man spoke with great sincerity.
He wished to share his good tidings
with somebody.
"My doctor" he said.
"My doctor has assured me
that providing I take my medication
at the appointed times
I will no longer feel like
whipping out my butcher's knife
in crowded lifts
and waving it around over my head.
Isn't that great?"
Then he looked at his watch.
"Oh shit" he said.

You have never heard a silence like it.

HIGH HEDGE EMPTY HOUSE

And a neighbour heard your cat meowing.

And the gardai saw you through your window
sitting in your chair.
When they got into your house
the cat ran up the stairs.

People were standing at your front gate.
They heard you had a sister in Canada or somewhere.
They heard you were sitting in your chair for three days.
They heard a lot of things.

A neighbour heard your cat meowing.

The gardai did the things that gardai have to do.
Then the ambulance.

Someone closed the front gate after them.

The chair is still there in the kitchen where you were sitting.
The vet came around about your cat.

Everything will stay exactly where it is
until your sister comes from Canada.
Or somewhere.

OH YES YES YES

A man told me yesterday
that chocolate
is a sex substitute.
Tomorrow I plan to enjoy
a multiple Malteser.

ME HOLD

They park buses
across the road
at night
in a flat place
because
there is no room
for them
in the garage.
Some nights
I would lie down
with them
for company.
Some nights
I would lie down
with railway carriages
in a siding.
Some nights
I would go
into the park
and lie down
with the trees.
Some nights
I would not go
anywhere.
I would lie down
alone.

My uncle Epiglottis
lovingly build a machine
with cogs and wheels
and chains and wires
and everything.
He walks up to it
and says
"What the hell do you
think you're looking at?"
And the machine replies
"I'm looking at you
your eyes are blue
your face is like
a kangaroo!"

Now that's what I call
an answering machine.

FOR MY GINGER FRIEND

Willow
you are the only one
who never lets me down.
No matter what people say
or don't say
or do
or don't do
you are here.
You don't know
how to hurt me.
I wish that I was
as much a man
as you are a cat.
I wish that I was
a cat.
I wish.

ON THIRD THOUGHTS

A butterfly zig-zags
all over the place
because all the time
it's thinking
"It's this way
ah no shit
it's that way
ah fuck no
it's the other way
hang on maybe
it's up here
ah shite no
I think it's
down there."

I blame their mothers.

IF YOU DON'T TELL ANYBODY I WON'T

I saw a man from the Waterboard
opening up a shore in Eyre Square
and putting a T-shaped bar
down into it
and twisting it around.
At least I thought
I saw a man from the Waterboard
until he motioned me over
and whispered
"Don't tell anybody
but right now
I am actually winding up
every clock in Galway."

HOW WILL YOU EVER GET OUT?

Two giant building site cranes
faced one another
across a vast black and white
squared chess board.
At the controls
of each crane
sat a chess master.
All the giant pieces
on the board were hollow.
Inside each one
sat two pregnant women
playing Chinese chequers.
The entire arena was enclosed
in an enormous perspex bubble
which zig-zagged around
inside the cracked thoughts
of Henry McGee.

Sometimes a woman cycles
out of an old calendar
and appears on Vernon Avenue.
She is riding
a high upright creaky bike
with a wicker basket on the front.
She is sitting up very straight
and looks neither to the left
or the right of her.
She is wearing a brown headscarf
and no bright colours.
She cycles up and up the avenue
in a perfectly straight line
and disappears into an old diary
when nobody is looking.

EARTH ME

I want to rub the juice of crushed grass all over my body
and feel what happens.
I want to press the skin of my bare feet down against wet sand
and let the water force its way up between my toes
and feel what happens.
I want to fall naked into a brambly bush.
I want to lie flat and let the shadow of a cloud
move across my body.
I want the sudden sun off the water to blind me.
I want to have so much
and feel so much
that is of the earth
and juice
and sharp
and wet
and wild
and me.

SOME LITTLE GIRLS GRIP DOORHANDLES WITH THEIR TEETH THEREBY COMPLETELY GIVING THE WRONG IMPRESSION

"Is she paralysed from the waist up?"

"No . . . she does Irish dancing."

Brocklesby Bracken hid in the bushes
at the side of the railway tracks
and he watched
and he waited
and with eyes to see
he saw it.
At four in the morning
some of the huge metal pylons
out in the fields
began to swing their arms
and twirl their electric wires
round and round
and chant –
"All in together girls
never mind the weather girls
get your hats
get your coats
get your umbrellas girls."
And the cows in the fields
had the time of their lives
skipping
until the sun came up.

GOING UP THE STAIRS IN BEWLEYS OF CORK 27-4-95

Oh God
the sparkles in the steps of the stairs
send me spinning this way and that
until I am afraid to look at them.
When I reach the top
I am higher and crazier
than the stairs is.

Just when my feet
are landing on the ground
a woman walks past me
with silver sparkles
in her sweater.
Everything is coming apart.

I THINK OF YOU

I moved the palm of my hand
to and fro across my forehead
and the friction
of skin upon skin
fired hot sparks
which burned the names
of my grandparents
into rough wood.

"PATRICK – BRIDIE
ELLEN – PADDY."

ON THE TRAIN TO WEXFORD 18-5-95

The countryside is swollen with so much green
that you could drown yourself in it
if you had a mind to.
All the trees and the grass and the bushes
at the side of the railway tracks
are saying to the telegraph pole
"We remember you".
They have clothed it with ivy
and they are saying – "Come on
– be one of us . . . again."

A sunken log is stabbing the river
with a black branch.
The high clouds are making maps
of new countries.
My train is going much too fast.

His face was brown from the sun and black from the coal yard and fear moved around inside my stomach every time he walked past our house. He moved along with quick little busy steps the way that our toy walking horse went when you stood it on a slanting book. I was afraid that he would look at me and smile because you felt very strange whenever he did that. There was something underneath the smile and the coal dust and the sun brown that made you feel like he was sucking you into him.

So I knelt behind the net curtain with my nose up against it and smelt the damp and I watched him walking very busy past our house. When he was gone the fear stayed in my stomach for a while and then it went away.

The coal yard felt safe when he wasn't in it. You could look in through the high iron-barred gate and see the big black sliding mountains of shiny coal. You could smell gas. The rough grey wall around the yard felt cold when you put your hand flat against it even when the sun was making tar soft on the road.

When he walked through a place it became cold. When he walked through a place the colours went out of it. The grey dust track outside our front gate. Three steps across it and your bare feet were feeling grass on the village green. The wind off the estuary would be blowing into your hair. The water was green and the water was blue and when it was blue it flowed into the sky. Village green and sea green and sky blue and when he walked past it was all gone.

The coal yard felt safe when he wasn't in it.

MISTER TOMMY

Didn't he stand at the corner
for long years
didn't he stand at the corner
and sniff the wind
and jiggle his weight
from one foot to the other
didn't he just.

Didn't he call everybody "Mister Tommy"
every man woman and child who passed
didn't he call them "Mister Tommy"
didn't he just.
"Do you think that they'll come today
Mister Tommy?
Do you think that they'll come"?

All the standing
all the jiggling up and down
sniffing the wind
and watching the railway bridge
when everyone was gone
to work to shop to town to sea
watching the bridge
"That's the way they'll come
Mister Tommy
That's the way they'll come."

Nobody is "Mister Tommy" anymore.
Nobody is keeping the watches.
They can come now
anytime they want to.

WHO?

Did you hear about Paddy?

Who?

You know . . . Pat.

Who?

PATRICK!

Oh . . . Patrick . . .
why didn't you say that?
. . . No.

He got cancer.

Go way.

They had to cut that much
of him away
all that was left was his ear
on the pillow.

Jaysus.

Now they're talking about
removing the ear as well.

Go way.

Sure there'll be nothing
of him left.

Poor Patrick.

Who?

Pat.

Who?

PADDY!

Oh.

A PARABLE FROM THE STREETS told to me by Mick

I went into the G.P.O.
to try and get me money a day early.

"Do you want it?" sez the girl.
"I do" sez I.

"Do you really want it?" sez the girl.
"I do" sez I.

"Yes but do you need it?" sez the girl.

You'd think I was askin' for me hole.

SUCK BLOW

When I was little
and lived beside the village green
in Malahide
there was a huge gasometer in the coal yard
which would rise and fall
according to how much gas was in it.

The Dublin Mountains are doing exactly
the same thing.
Don't tell me they're not – because they are.
The Dublin Mountains are going up and down
according to how much mountain is in them.
Some force or some power
with a huge big hosepipe
is pumping more mountain in
or sucking it out.
God alone knows why.
You could always ask somebody.

THEY PROBABLY WON'T SEE THIS EITHER
SO THEY WON'T

They tell me
when they don't see me
on television they do.

"I don't see much of you
on the telly these days
so I don't."

They tell me
when they don't hear me
on the radio they do.

"I don't hear much of you
on the radio these days
so I don't."

They tell me
when they don't see me
in the papers they do.

"I don't see much of you
in the papers these days
so I don't."

If they ever read this poem
I earnestly request them
to tell me that they didn't
so I do.

HELP HIM

Lurching along North Earl Street
well-dressed well-spoken
and drunk
roaring very loud
"WE'RE ALL SUPPOSED
TO HELP ONE ANOTHER".
Roaring fear into three children
who move close together.
Roaring fear into an old nun
who ducks back into The Kylemore
and stays there.
Roaring fear into the sun
which snuffs behind a cloud.
Roaring fear into James Joyce
who looks the other way.
Roaring around the corner
into O'Connell Street
where the crowd drowns him.

A pigeon lands on the silence.

GINGERBREAD MEN – THE WAY THEY MIGHT LOOK AT YOU

God – I couldn't bite his head off.
I just couldn't.
I was hungry and everything
and his head was covered in chocolate
and he looked delicious
but he had this pink smile
iced onto the chocolate
and he was grinning at me
so I said – "O.K. then – how about
if I bite off one of your legs instead?"
and he just looked at me
so I bought a ham roll
because they don't have heads or legs
or pink smiles iced onto them.
Maybe the pig had though.

BREAKING POINT

My word processor said to me very politely
"Insert a sheet of paper O.K."
29,361 times consecutively.
I counted them.

On the 29,362nd time it said
"PUT IN SOME PAPER YOU FUCKWIT."
Put it in yourself if you're so smart.

GONE FOR GOOD

The teacher said
"Come up to the blackboard Hennessy
and give us the benefit of your great knowledge.
Point out the continent of Africa."

Hennessy walked up and stared at the map
for a very long time.
We watched and waited and willed him to find it.
We felt the room growing cold with our stomachs.

"My God Hennessy don't tell me you can't
do that either."

"I had it a minute ago sir but it's gone now."

I don't think that it ever came back.

Sir.

NO HARM DONE

The white ambulance shrieked around Dublin
with a siren so sharp and so shrill
that it cut peoples' ears off.
Then it picked them all up
and rushed them to hospital
where their ears were sewn back on again
in exactly the right order. Proper.

I LOVE DUBLIN (1)

I walked into Anne's Bakery and Restaurant.

"Will you give me a gingerbread man called Kevin please?"

"Sorry Pat – they're all called Jason."

I LOVE DUBLIN (2)

Bright lights, cameras and excitement on Pearse Station.
They are making a film about Michael Collins.
Actors and actresses are pretending to be Dubliners.
Metal barriers are holding the real Dublin people back.
Three little kids are jumping up and down and laughing
and having great crack.

"Hey misther – how much is it into the show?"

"It's not a show – it's a film."

"C'mon – we'll go home an' watch it on the telly.
Hey misther – what channel is it on?"

I LOVE DUBLIN (3)

I was buying a can of Finches Sparkling Orange.

"Eh – do they liquidise birds or what . . . you know like
. . . finches?'

"Jaysus no Pat . . . the finches don't break down well . . .
you get beaks and claws in the drink . . . no . . .
they use pigeons instead."

I LOVE DUBLIN (4)

A young school girl approached me
rattling her collection tin.

"Will you help Ardscoil Eanna please?
It burnt down."

"God that's terrible – was anybody hurt?"

"Eh . . . it didn't actually . . . it's just . . . people give
you more money when you say that."

EITHER WAY NO WAY OUT CONNOLLY STATION
29-5-1995

Lots of people
are rising up
out of the concrete
across the railway tracks
on Platform Six.
Men and women
rising up sideways
from left to right
the tips of their heads
the right side of their faces
necks
shoulders
rising
up and up
and out
Platform Six
creating
shaping
men and women
whole people
to satisfy the trains.

Other people
lots of other people
men and women
are slanting down
sideways
into the hard grey
right to left
sinking
the tips of their feet
trouser legs
further still
sideways
swallowing down
as far as the waist

further still
no redemption
the tips of their heads
gone.

A heavy green train slides away
on silver iron
underneath its electric cobweb.
Already
framed in every window
you can see what remains.
People from the waist up
riding the rails
to where they slice the sky
and fling them
into infinity.

A BIOGRAPHICAL NOTE THAT YOU'LL NEVER READ ON THE BACK OF A POETRY BOOK.

Nigel Wetherby won the Clifford Pilkington-Whyte Poetry Prize in 1976, 1977 and 1978 because he was the only one who entered a poem.

He won the Bryan Henderson Gold Medal in 1978 and 1979 because Henderson was screwing his mother.

He has read his poems in Russia. They couldn't understand them either.

This is his third book.

The other two are shite.

This one is worse.

OH GAVIGAN

Gavigan Whipsnade reached across Dublin Bay
and lifted Howth Head up
with his finger and his thumb
to let a bit of air in under it.

"I wouldn't do that if I was you" said the man
beside him on the DART. "Now all the maps
of Ireland are wrong."

"By God you're right" said Gavigan. "And my son
is doing his geography this afternoon."

So he put it straight back again.

WHERE CREDIT IS DUE

My granny knew and she told us.
"There's nothing good out after midnight"
that's what my granny said.

All the robbers and ruffians and rogues
footpads and forgers
bowsies and brigands
sneakthieves and snatchers
all waiting inside their front doors
all looking at their watches
"No . . . no . . . don't go yet
it's a minute to midnight.
Pat's granny will be raging."

And that's how the West was won.

SOMETHING LOVELY HAPPENED TODAY
North Earl Street 27-6-95

And me sitting in the street
the sun red-roasting my arms
me reading a poem
black printed on a bright white page
a poem which is telling me
"Look deep into ordinary things
and you will transform them."

A fly lands on the page
split-second
and stays there
beside the black print of the poem
and I am looking deep into it.

See how the sun is lighting through its wings
and throwing two little transparent shadows
onto the page.
See how the slight breeze is ruffling
its tiny twin antennae.
See how it clings to my page.

I am sitting in the city street
this tiny insect and its shadow on my page
are the centre of my universe
for as long as I choose to delight in them
or until it flies away.

NOW YOU DON'T

Pigeons come out of nowhere
they really do.
They suddenly appear
out of nothing
and drop onto the pavement.
"Hi everybody – I'm here!"
I believe that they burst
out of invisible Time Tunnels.
One minute they are grooving
around in Ancient Rome
peeping up senators' togas.
Next thing they are flapping
for their lives because The DART
is trying to run them down
at Connolly Station.
It is very confusing for a pigeon.
You don't know where the hell
you are.
You can't plan ahead or anything.
"The French Revolution?
How the fuck did I get here –
I was outside Clerys a minute ago."

I know the feeling.

When the old man with the woollen hat
started talking out loud to himself
in the ILAC Library
and the echoes took his voice
all around the books
and all around my head
I got a feeling of cold fright
and twenty five years ago
was right now
and right now
was Ward 3b
and the old man with the woollen hat
was talking to himself
in the dark
and he was awake
and other old men
were talking to themselves
and they were asleep
and Ward 3b was filled with old mens' voices
all talking out loud to themselves
and I could not get away from them.
That is why I left the ILAC Library
in a hurry without a book
and walked very quickly
up Henry Street
and did not stop walking for a very long time.
One old man talking to himself in a library
can put the cold hand back inside you
and fill your head with voices.
One old man can waken up 3b.
I do not know how to make it sleep.

STILL

I am standing deep in the silence
outside my front door.
Day has dipped into dark.
Nothing makes a sound.
The edges of night
are back-lit by slight blue.
Leaves hang limp
in the shadow shape of trees.
A seagull passes over
like a black movement
and disturbs nothing.
If I stay here like this
I will live forever.

ARTS IT TO DEATH

I know it's called 'The Summer Arts Show'
but for Christ's sake don't answer his questions.

Play your music.

It is wild, untamed and fills me full of crazy fire.

Ignore his questions about finger styling and phrasing.

Tell him to go and dismantle a refrigerator.
Tell him to analyse a plastic dustbin.
Tell him as quickly and briefly as possible.
Then play your music.

Play it. Celebrate it before his six-inch questions
nail it to the floor.

THRILL

Your hungry tongue
is wriggling around
inside my mouth
like a pleasure seeking
fish.
Now you are thrusting
and flicking
and touching the tip
of my tongue
with the tip
of yours
and thrilling me
with tiny tips
towards the point
of sweet explosion.

Oh – let it go!

HARVEST

I have just cleared a space on my floor.
It is ready to receive 2000 more copies
of "POEMS SO FRESH AND SO NEW
– YAHOO!"
The van arrives at 9 o'clock tomorrow
morning.
I will help the man.
Together we will walk
           in and out
           in and out
           to the van.
He will wheel
and I will carry.
We will sweat.
My forehead
under my arms
will be wet.
It will be worth it.

When he has gone
I will look at
my new blue and white
book mountain
all along the wall
of my sitting-room
and say to myself
"Here we go again."

David my nephew will ferry
them upstairs.
It is hot tiring work.
He is young and strong.
I will give him £20.
It will be worth it.

My small room upstairs
is my treasure house.

One mountain
purple and black.
"HOW WAS IT FOR YOU
DOCTOR?"
One mountain
blue and white
"POEMS SO FRESH AND SO NEW
– YAHOO!"

My poems.
I write them.
I publish them.
I love them.
They keep me alive.
I sell them through the shops.
I sell them in the streets.
My face and my arms
are brown from the sun.

Tonight I will lie awake
for a long time. Excited.
Like Christmas Eve.
A long time ago.
My books are coming
in the morning.

He was more than a little surprised to discover
that when he took his shoes off
his feet came away as well.

She was more than a little surprised to discover
that when she pushed her sunglasses
onto the top of her head
her eyes went up with them.

He was more than a little surprised to discover
that when he drew his stomach in suddenly
his feet exploded.

She was more than a little surprised to discover
that when she pressed her left nipple
the church bells rang.

He was more than a little surprised to discover
that when the doctor removed his appendix
there was graffiti written on it.

She was more than a little surprised to discover
that when she lay down to sleep
her toes whispered secrets to one another
under the covers.

He was more than a little surprised to discover
that everytime he did a wee wee
his vocabulary grew smaller.

She was more than a little surprised to discover
that when she pricked herself with a thorn
her name came out.

He was more than a little surprised to discover
that his memory was still waiting for permission
to get started.

She was more than a little surprised to discover
that her shadow touched wet flowers
ten seconds before she did.

He was more than a little surprised to discover
that fear from his childhood
made the candle go out.

She was more than a little surprised to discover
that her new-born baby had a handle
in the middle of his back and wheels
underneath each foot.

He was more than a little surprised to discover
that she knew all these things about him
before he told her.

She wasn't.

TOUCH

I placed my hand gently
on the wet red and yellow rose
and cupped it against my palm.
I felt my skin touching
soft wet petals.
I stood there for a very long time
until once again
I could feel the rise and fall
of my breathing
and there was peace in me.

MAKE STRAIGHT THE CROOKED PATHS –
HERE COMES THE DOCTOR

She was telling me about her sister
in hospital.
Everytime she mentioned the specialist
she genuflected with her voice.

She was telling me about herself.
"Of course – I married a dentist.
We have three sons.
An orthodontist, a paediatrician
and a gynaecologist."

So who brings in the coal from the bunker?

A TEACOSY ON HER HEAD –
A MESSAGE TO THE WORLD

Oh Miss Brady
what a great thing you taught us.
Not two times tables
though they were good enough.
Not the poem about six ducks
though they were good too.
Oh Miss Brady
the day you silenced our class
the day you hushed us
        and shushed us
because you knew
that we were ready.

"Now class – what I am about
to tell you – you must never forget.
What must you never do?"

"Forget, Miss."

"I am only going to say this once.
How often am I going to say it?"

"Once, Miss."

She paused.
She straightened her teacosy.
The dusty sunbeams spun
The Holy Spirit into her.
She spoke.

"MY DEAR CHILDREN OF GOD.
EVERYTIME YOU CROSS YOUR LEGS
YOU GET YOUR GUTS TANGLED."

We were amazed.
We were astonished.

We were speechless.

"WHAT HAPPENS WHEN YOU CROSS YOUR LEGS?"

"You get your guts tangled, Miss."

"HOW DO YOU GET YOUR GUTS TANGLED?"

"You cross your legs, Miss."

"AND DON'T YOU FORGET IT!"

Her spot checks were sudden and terrifying.
She grabbed us from behind in the playground
and yelled – "CROSSED LEGS?"

"Tangled guts" we responded.

She sprang out from behind trees
in the park and shrieked
"TANGLED GUTS?"

"Crossed legs" we responded.

Oh Miss Brady
I present to you a coat of arms.
Three dusty sunbeams
illuminating in turn
one pair of crossed legs
one tangled gut
and a teacosy.
Oh Miss Brady
I remember you.
Oh Miss Brady
how I remember.

SINGULAR

I think that doctors should only ask
"And how are we this morning?"
when they are addressing the occupants
of a double bed.

HE HAS NO WORDS FOR IT

Me and Mairead are talking to one another
in the street.
She is finger-tipping her words onto the keyboard
in front of her.
We're having a brilliant chat.
As Mairead types her words they appear on a little screen
and a metallic voice says them out loud.
A man is standing nearby.
He is watching and listening.
He is afraid to come forward so I say to him
"This is my friend Mairead."
"Nice to meet you Mairead" he says and smiles.
"Although I don't know why you're talking to a fool like that."
This is the only way he knows how to communicate.
This is his vocabulary of love at work.
When he is gone Mairead finger-tips a message to me,.
"We are not fools."
How right you are Mairead. How right you are.

The poor man.

FOR WHAT CAN NEVER BE AGAIN

Sometimes I am lying awake in the dark
feeling very much alone
and I hear the television next door
and I pretend that it is a long time ago
and my parents are downstairs
listening to the wireless
and I feel lovely and safe.
Tears come up inside me.
Then I sleep.

SOME OF THE THINGS THAT PEOPLE SAID TO ME
WHILE I WAS SELLING MY POETRY BOOKS
ON THE STREET

"Are you doin' that for Pat Ingoldsby . . . are you sellin' his books for him?"

"Nobody has no money . . . wha?"

"What do you want to make more money for? You're loaded."

WOMAN POINTING TO HER DAUGHTER: "She thought you were dead."

"What did ye blow all your money on? We all blow it on somethin'. Was it the powder or wha"?

"Do ye know wha' Pat . . . livin' out in Phibsboro has me head wrecked. People washin' cars and diggin' gardens. Sure I'm not used to tha."

"I find it a little extraordinary to see you here selling your books."

"Are you Your Man? A Hundred Coats or something?"

"Sometimes I go into Easons and stand there readin' your books and I do burst me shite laughin.' "

"I recognise you by your shape . . . you're Pat Ingoldsby aren't you."

"You should be up in Grafton Street."

"You should be over in America."

"You should take that hat off and get a bit of sun."

"You should put natural yoghurt on your feet."

"You should get a big umbrella and keep the sun off you."

"You should get a couple of kids to stand beside you."

"Why don't you hold up a load of coloured balloons wha?"

"My girlfriend read one of your poems to me on the phone from Bankok at ten o'clock this morning."

"I had seven kids Pat and then I found out what was causing it."

"What's this? Second-hand books or wha?"

"I only got arrested for street trading once. I got probation for selling balloons."

"I got your book here last week. There's a lot of dirt in it but I liked it."

"I married an ex-mot of yours and I got divorced three years ago."

"Do you not think you're wastin' yourself all the same? You were very good with the kids."

"You've got a bit thin have you? You look young or something."

"You never put my pictures on the telly."

"You're only a bollix."

AS FAR AS I CAN BE SURE IT'S A BIT OFF
WEDNESDAY THE 19TH OF APRIL 1995

There is a bit of daylight in my sitting-room.
It is about the size of a shoebox.
You'd really like it.
It has been there for about three months now.
Day and night.
Beside my beanbag.
It never goes away.
I think it is part of a Wednesday.
An abandoned bit.
It has a sort of a Wednesday look about it.
I cannot imagine why the Wednesday didn't want it.
It looks perfectly alright to me.
Perhaps another day will come along soon
and take it in.
I certainly hope so.
If I was a day myself I'd be delighted to fit it in.
In the meantime it is quite welcome to stay
exactly where it is.
Beside the beanbag.
It is not harming anyone.
Sometimes Willow and Hoot like to sleep in it.
That is alright too.
I have no objection to days dumping bits around
my house.
It's the nights I'm worried about.

TWO STEPS AHEAD

I watched the wasted pair of them
making their pricked and punctured way
down North Earl Street
and an open grave was moving along
in front.

HAIL TO THEE

Any seagull can hit Daniel O'Connell on top of the head.
There's nothing to it.
He's a statue. He's just standing there.
It's no big deal.
But the one who hit me today is a true artist.
A seagull amongst seagulls.
Absolutely majestic.
Whilst whooshing past
goodness knows how high up
it contrived to whack a shite against my shirt
and ricochet it sideways
and splat my canvas chair in two places.
That is three direct hits with one inspired shite.
I couldn't do that – not even if I was suspended
on a rope and practiced for months.

Seagull – I salute thee.
Your blood is worth bottling.
So indisputably is your shite.

We've got a grip on your heartbeat.
We've got the power of your pulse.
We will make you dance.
By God we will.
We will make you dance and jump
any way we want to.
We've got the power
and we like it.
The life of your limbs
the bubble of your blood
the sight of the lights
the jerk of your jumps
the heat of your heart
any way we want you.

We will send you home
when the music stops.
We can get you again
any how
any time
any place
any way we want to.

SKELETAL

Now I know what close to the bone means.
When I touch my left upper arm
with my finger
it hurts.
There is little flesh there.
Close to the bone.
When somebody touches my left upper arm
with their hand
it hurts.
There is little flesh there.
It frightens me.
Close to the bone.
Brittle stick.
Don't break.

I CAN'T STOP

My mind is seagull shaped
and high-speed swooping
over beaches
of twenty years ago.
I am hanging onto
the edges of my mattress
and waiting
for the crazy energy
of this night
to dump me
exhausted
onto the shores
of tomorrow morning.

A WAY TO GET YOUR HANDS ON LOTS AND LOTS OF MONEY WITHOUT USING GUNS OR KNIVES OR AWFUL THINGS LIKE THAT

Walk up to the counter of any bank of your choice.
Stick your finger into your ear.
Wiggle it around well.
Brandish it menancingly in the air.
Say to the cashier – "Hand over oodles and oodles
of money or I will TOUCH you with my earwax."
The teller may very well thrust her finger
up her nose
take it out again
brandish it in your direction and respond
"Put that earwax down
or you will force me to TOUCH you with THIS."

Be gracious in defeat.

ANOTHER WAY

Walk up to the back of a security van.
Knock briskly on the hatch.
It will open. A hand will reach out
and give you a bag of money.
It may however grab hold of you
fully and frontally instead.
Do not struggle.
It will only encourage him.

I GOT A MEDAL FOR MY CONFIRMATION BUT THAT
WAS DIFFERENT BECAUSE EVERYBODY GOT ONE

I think it is lovely to give a medal to a cow.
Any sort of a medal.
Cow Of The Year.
Cow With The Dreamiest Eyes.
     The Swishiest Tail.
     The Sweepiest Eyelashes.
I think it is daft to give a medal to a poet.
Any sort of a medal.
No matter how sweepy his eyelashes are.

I think it is lovely to give a prize to a fancy-dress contestant.
Any sort of a prize.
The One Who Looks Most Like Goofy.
          Charlie Chaplain.
          Lassie.
I think it is daft to give a prize to a poet.
Any sort of a prize.
Unless he can run faster
     jump higher
     or dive deeper
     than other poets.
In that case he probably deserves one.

HALL OF MIRRORS

The woman was smiling warmly
and walking towards me.
I felt good and excited.
I didn't realise that she was smiling
over my shoulder
at the man behind me.
The man behind me was smiling
towards the woman.
She didn't realise that he was smiling
over her shoulder
at the woman behind her.
The woman behind her was smiling
towards the man.
He didn't realise that she was smiling
to herself because she could see
exactly what was happening.

DAYS LIKE THESE

Today nobody is stopping.
Today nobody is buying.
It is as if I am invisible.
I do not understand it.
Other days people do stop.
Other days people do buy.
Today is a day like any other.
It is no different.
I am standing in the same place.
The weather is exactly the same.
I am exactly the same.
Yet today everybody is walking past.
Nobody is stopping.
Nobody is buying.
It is a complete mystery to me.
If you know the reason please tell me.
I would love to know.

A VAGUE HALF-FORMED AMBITION

To break into the National Wax Museum late one night
and melt myself with a blowlamp.

WHEEEEEE!!!

He took out his earrings and cycled downhill
at very high speed on his racing bike.
The wind whistled through the holes in his ears
and set up a high-pitched sonic signal
which disorientated bats, confused sheepdogs
and distorted the pictures on Arabella Quigley's
television.

He does that.

SECURE OH MY SECURE

"This vehicle is locked in such a way
  that nobody can ever get into it
  and the crew can never get out.
  In fact they will all eventually die
  in here."

So don't even think about it.

I always get a terrible fright
when old men whoosh
their bottom set of false teeth forward.
They do a funny sort
of contemplative chewing movement
which makes their bottom teeth rise up
and lurch outwards.
It scares the living daylights out of me.
I always think they are going to bite
a lump out of my leg.
I calm myself with the thought
that they can't bite me
without lunging and lurching
their top set as well.

When old men perfect that technique
when old men master the simultaneous
upper and lower lunge
we are in profoundly deep trouble.
Run for your life.

IT'S GREAT ALL THE SAME

The street juggler tossed his three blue clubs
high up into the air
and three rabbits fell down.

"Hang on a minute" one of the onlookers shouted.
"You planted those rabbits up there."

"How in the name of God could I do that?
They were probably flying too low."

"Oh – I see . . . well that's alright so."

Nobody noticed that the three clubs
never came down again.

ONE OF THE POEMS WHICH I WROTE IN MY LAST BOOK WAS WITH CHILD AND THAT'S WHERE THIS ONE CAME FROM

The hitchhiker was walking slower and slower.
She came to a stop beside me.
"My rucksack has grown heavier and heavier
over the past few weeks" she said.
"I think it is with child."

Next morning she walked sprightly past.
A brand new holdall skipped along
beside her.
"I was hoping for a sleeping bag" she said.
"But thanks be to God anyway."
Indeed.

DA YOU IN YOUR BEAUTY

My father leaning forward in his chair
cupping his hand against his ear
helping it to hear what they are saying
on the television.
My father watching something very gentle
and beaming with open pleasure
smiling his delight
not knowing if anyone is watching him
and caring less.
Today I catch myself doing exactly
the same thing.
For a moment I am he.
His spent bits lie deep underground
in Malahide.
His wondrous love of beauty
lives on in me.

The air is very warm and doesn't move inside the tent.
The high sun is touching the canvas with strong heat.
I am standing beside the open flap
and looking into the green dome.
Circus people are sitting on the wooden steps
outside their caravans.
A man is carrying a silver bucket full of water.
They are not minding me.
I am looking into their empty green cave
and wandering my eyes
around the curve of the wooden ring
the curve of the seats.
A horse is pulling grass with its teeth
and I can hear the grass breaking.
There is no other sound.
Just me and the green dome
and the silence
when circus people are at rest
and a little boy is amazed.

Tomorrow they will be gone.

CHILL

Iceberg
rough white diamond
sunlight splinters
where it hits
flinging spears of light
back towards the sun.
Ice hard diamond
out of sight
behind my eyes
turning them to glass
freezing me to death.

SELL-BY DATE ON CONDOM

Best before ejaculation.

TOGETHER AGAIN

He watched with astonishment while it happened.
The top half of him from his waist up
slid very slowly sideways towards the right.
The bottom half of him from his waist down
slid very slowly sideways towards the left
and he parted company with himself.
The top half mystified people
by resting in extremely shallow water
at the beach and shouting "Help!"
The bottom half scampered around the Phoenix Park
and disrupted soccer matches.
The top half rested on the sand and said
"Will somebody please dig me out of here?"
The bottom half stood behind toilet doors
so that nobody knew the difference.
The top half sat on a skateboard
and whizzed down a ski slope.
The bottom half ran in under a horse
and out the other side.
The top half rested beside the bottom half
on an altar in Christchurch Cathedral
while the Dean joined them together again
and pronounced them man.

The old man didn't want any more.
He'd had enough.
He stood in front of a wall
and said – "Take me"
but nothing happened.
He tried again.
"Receive me."
Nothing happened.
So he stood in front of a bus.

THINKER

"How much is your book?" asked the man.

"Five ninety five."

"Oh . . . I see . . . I'll eh . . . I'll just go away for a while
and have a serious think about it."

That was over three hours ago.
My God – I hope he's alright.
I hope that he's not crouching alone
in a secluded alleyway
concentrating so deeply
that clammy sweat and muted moans
are leaking out of him.

If he comes back today
I am going to give him a book for nothing.
He has earned it.

When the bin bags are flung into the lorry
how they scream.
Oh my how they scream.
When the hard metal teeth press down on them
how they shriek
oh my how they shriek.
When the whiskey, gin and vodka bottles
are hung upside down behind the bar
how they groan.
Oh my how they groan.
When an empty glass is pushed up underneath
and the pressure is relieved
how they sigh with relief.
It is lovely.
Oh my how lovely.

She stood before me
holding a blank sheet of cardboard.

"Are you doing 'the hungry and homeless' '?

She nodded. "Yeah but I don't know the words.
Will you write them out on a bit of paper?"

I printed it very clearly in block capitals.
"HUNGRY AND HOMELESS.
PLEASE HELP ME."

"Will you give me the lend of your pen"?

I did.

Off she went with the cardboard, the paper, my pen.

Ten minutes later she stood before me again
and held up the cardboard.

"Is that the right words?"

"It is."

And off she went to beg.

SOME MORE OF THE THINGS THAT PEOPLE SAID
TO ME WHILE I WAS SELLING MY
POETRY BOOKS ON THE STREET

"God it's only poetry . . . would you not write a nice story or something?"

"Me oul flower . . . how did you go as low as this?"

"Where can I get the words of 'Who Fears To Speak of '98"?

"I'm stuck for a couple of pounds – I think I'll go down to the College of Surgeons and donate me pussy."

"Weren't you famous once?"

"Fair play to you Pat – you're a great trier."

"I just want to tell you – you're wrong about everything."

"I just want to say – I agree with you on the telly and that. People think you're an idiot and that, you know."

"Your hair was better long."

"Do you see that man . . . have a good look at him. That's Pat Ingoldsby. In about three years he'll be famous."

"You have it handy sitting there you lucky bastard."

"How much is your book?"
"Five ninety five."
"Jaysus – I'll get it in the library."

"Keep an eye on that bike will you."

"I used to like you until you went all scruffy."

"I bought one last week and it's brilliant. Give us two more."

"Lend us a pound."

"Our class was talking about you in school. All the girls loved your poems but one girl said – 'He's a reject from the Sixties who got lost.' The teacher was raging."

"Do you know what brought down Henry the Second? The gargle. He stopped all the drink for his troops. "Get over to France an' fight' he sez." "But yiz are gettin' no more drink." And they said "Fuck this . . . you can fight your own war."

"I'm from New Zealand. My father told me to say hello to you. He met you here last year."

"Amn't I right in thinking you took a turn or something?"

"I can't buy a book because I haven't got me trousers on and me money is in me sock."

BRUTAL

The worst singer in the whole world
was busking near me in the street today.
She was determined to make each song
wish that it had never been written.
Her chain-saw voice hacked through
corrugated metal.
Her jagged screech ripped the gizzard out of pigeons.
Her sharp scream pitched agony
into suicidal eardrums.
At its very finest
her voice would remind you
of a wild row between two axes
inside an empty washing-machine.
At its very worst
her voice would remind you of a crash between two
grinding pains.
When it rose to a terrible pitch
the feathers fell off seagulls.

When she stopped singing
it was lovely.
The silence.
Lovely.
People came back to the street
for weeks afterwards
just to listen to it.
The silence.
Lovely.

A THOUGHT WHICH OCCURRED TO ME ON THE 9TH AUGUST 1995 AS I WAS SITTING IN NORTH EARL STREET SELLING MY BOOKS

Someday all the people who stop
and look at my books and say
"I'll catch you on the way back"
someday all those people
will come back together
at exactly the same time
and unintentionally
trample me to death.
Then my books will really
start to sell.

WHOOSH

He was walking along the street
picking his nose so vigorously
that he suddenly found himself
standing on a window ledge
two floors up.

I WOULD BE LOST WITHOUT THEM

When I was growing up
there was always someone
in the house.
Michael, Ann, David, Brigid,
my mother and father.
There was always someone there.
The house is rented now.
Strangers live in it.
My father lies in a silent corner
of the old Malahide cemetery.
My mother is in a nursing home.
She doesn't know what day it is.
David is in Canada.
Ann is in Africa.
Michael is somewhere with Fossett's Circus.
Brigid is in Firhouse.
Sooty, Cheffy, Sarah, Volks, Centuries
and all the other cats are a long time dead.
So is Snowy the rabbit
and Alfred and Ruben the hedgehogs.
Everybody smiles out of old brown photographs.
When I lie down at night in my bedroom
there is nobody else in my house.
After a while in the darkness
I feel Willow and Hoot moving onto the mattress
beside me.
I thank God that they are there.

THE REAL REASON WHY THE COMPETITION IN THE BUTCHERS' DEPARTMENT WAS DECLARED NULL AND VOID AND DON'T LET ANYBODY EVER TELL YOU OTHERWISE

Because no matter how carefully
the contestants
attempted to reassemble a cow
no matter how ingeniously
they put the pieces back together
no matter how persistently
they squeezed and wobbled
their entries
they could not make them
"Moo."

ACROSS THE YARD

Valentine Duff is walking across the yard
and I know where he is going.
He is going to kill a cow.
Valentine Duff is walking across the yard
with a T-shaped gun in his hand.
When he goes into the small slaughter house
the cow will look at him.
I am standing across the yard
looking at the wooden door.
I know as soon as he has done it
because there is a different kind of silence.
Valentine Duff is walking back across the yard.
I am afraid to look at him.

THIS IS WHY I DIDN'T TURN UP LAST NIGHT HONEST TO GOD IT IS CROSS MY HEART AND HOPE TO DIE

Because the bus was speeding along
and the road was disappearing
in under the front of it
but it wasn't coming out again
at the back
so when the bus reached its
destination it wasn't able
to make the return journey
because the road was gone.

WHILE I'M AT IT THIS IS WHY I DIDN'T PHONE

Because I closed my mouth too quickly
and my lower jaw kept on going up
and swallowed my head.

WEIRD

The reflection of our carriage
outside my window
showed me the man
behind the next seat
who did not know
that I was looking out
into his mirror sunglasses
and sharing his silver vision.

A POEM IN DEEP ADMIRATION FOR THOSE BRILLIANT GREEN AND BUSHY PLANTS WHICH SOMEHOW MANAGE TO GROW OUT OF THE SIDES OF BUILDINGS VERY HIGH UP EVEN THOUGH THERE IS NO SOIL WHATSOEVER UP THERE AND GOD ALONE KNOWS HOW THEY GET THEIR ROOTS INTO THOSE TEENCHY LITTLE CRACKS IN THE BRICKWORK

My dear green and bushy plants,
during my black and barren periods
when the only thing I wish to do
is fall asleep and never wake up again
I wander around Dublin City
looking towards the tops
of incredibly high buildings
and when I see you sprouting out
of a truly impossible place
where you have no right to be
I quietly murmur – "If you guys
can make it up there
well maybe perhaps down here
I can cling on too."
Thank you.

CIRCUS DRIVING IN THE SPIKES

When the men swung their heavy hammers
up and round and down upon the spikes
the agony of metal striking metal
shrieked around the sky
and scarcely died
before another hammer swung
up and round and down
driving spikes deep into the ground.
Hot wet shiny men icing the sky
with the sound of metal striking.
And after the echoes of the last strike
shivered into silence
there came a deep edge
which held the men
motionless
amazed
a split-second
between the last spike
and silencing the silence.

CIRCUS HAULING UP THE CANVAS

The men ran with the canvas
rolled it flat along the grass
green segments
canvas slices
waiting to be stitched
waiting for the men
to rope them
thread them
bind them tight together
tie them to the pulleys
and haul them into life
hand over hand
rising
jerking
creaking
becoming pregnant
with the wind
fighting with the men
all the way towards
the triumph at the top.

Henry Humble was crouched down
in the late-night lane
listening to the black plastic bags
telling him their secrets
when the cracks between the paving stones
rose up with matchstick leaps and skinny skips
and already they knew his name.
"Come 'ere Henry Humble.
Come 'ere – we want you!"
"God as my witness" he said
with river water still on his lips.
"God as my witness – I jumped the wall
and hid under the Liffey."
And who pulled you out?
Nobody
yet.

FROM WHERE INTO WHAT?

I was walking down Vernon Avenue to do my shopping
and inside my mind was a crystal clear picture
of the upper deck on a 15A bus moving along Dawson Street.
When I looked up into the ceiling I could see the reflections
of upside down pedestrians standing on their heads.
One of them reached into his pocket and pulled out his hanky.
A shower of coins cascaded down into the lap of a woman
who hadn't got her bus fare.
I looked onto the pavement in Vernon Avenue
and it was littered with pennies and twopenny pieces.
The ones she didn't need.

ATTEMPTED ROBBERY IN BEWLEYS

The man raced up to the girl at the cash register.

"Hand over all the money" he said.
"I've got a gun."

"Loaded or unloaded?"

"Loaded."

"Handgun or shotgun?"

"Handgun. Now come on! The money!"

"Notes or coins?"

"Notes."

"Loose or with a rubber band?"

"Go an' ask me granny."

When she returned
he was in protective custody
refusing to answer
any more questions.

A patient line of men and women queued quietly
in between the blue ropes of the obedient bank.
One of the men entered much much deeper
into a sheep dipping fantasy
than was advisable for him to go.
As he plunged into the cold dip
he released a wild series of frightened bleats.
There were six of them in rapid succession.
"BA BA BA BA BA BA."
The echoes had scarcely died
before every man and woman
raised their woolly heads
and sent up such a rising blitz of bleats
that the manager came face to face
with his fulfilment.
With sweet alacrity
he slipped into his smock
with keen authority
he tightly grasped his crook.
The words when they came
were swift and sure and true.
"HUP HUP HUP HUP, HUP HUP."
Merrily he hupped
and happily he herded.
Peacefully they grazed upon the green
while the manager embraced
the inner shepherd
someplace in-between.

Black and brown marks on her legs
secretive
unsteady
wet on her lips
alcohol
in a city
Glasgow
on a station
Queen Street
sitting down
shaky beside me.
"What's your name?"
"Pat."
"Where you from?"
"Dublin."
She goes down deep
into her eyes.
Wipes her lips.
"What's your name?"
"Pat."
"Where you from?"
"Dublin."
She looks into her can.
"What's your name?"
"Pat."
"Where you from?"
"Dublin."
She sees something
in her finger.
She tells it things.
She hears something
inside her can
and waits for it
to go away.
"What's your name?"
"Pat."
"Where you from?"

"Dublin."
What's your name
old lady?
Where you from?
She goes deep
into her eyes
and loses herself.
I touch her shoulder
and walk away.

The song I heard when we threw shells
up into the air and laughed at reflected light.
The same song when seagulls huddled near us
on a rock and we breathed quietly to watch them.
You brushing your hair long and each sweep
of the brush sent down ripples to your shoulders.
Our feet on springy turf, erratic rock,
and back to turf again.
God – how I miss you.
I miss you again and again and again.
I am afraid to speak your name in my mind
because this train is full of people.
I am afraid to think about the song.
When I get home to Ireland
I will draw my curtains
and listen to it on the tape
and nobody will see me.

STARTING TO FEEL CLOSE AND RIGHT AND THERE IS EXCITEMENT AND RECOGNITION IN IT

My pis was showering
onto the sand
and frothing down
to meet the waves
foaming up
and when one flowed
into the other
after a moment
I could no longer tell
which was which.

ONCE ON SAND

I see now again how it was.
Waves moving shells at the wet edge.
Seaweed twisted high the way the tide left it.
A piece of sky trapped in a crooked pool.
I was seeing in your eyes for the very first time
and you were seeing in my eyes
and I did not look away
and you did not look away
and for a quiet while
I was glad.

I'D RATHER BE A HORSE

People
Milk producers in particular
really should not
pick cows up by their tails
and whizz them
round and round in the air
and send them skittering away
across the surface
of inland lakes and waterways.

Let us together
seek out and find
more humane ways
of producing
skimmed milk
than this.

EXTRACT FROM A TOMBSTONE AT GLASGOW CATHEDRAL

Doctor Peter Law. 1612.
"He got the grace
to live in mirth
and die in peace."

Well lucky you.

Grey face
pale face
little boy
surrounded.
Ring of poison
fingers point
fingers jab
"Arsehole"
"Dirtbird"
"Dickhead"
"Shite".
Words to hurt
       bruise
       cut
       stab
and drive him
   into dark.
The agony on the bus.
Brave boy
surrounded.
Even from the path
they shout it
through the windows.
"Arsehole"
"Dirtbird"
"Dickhead"
"Shite".
He doesn't run.
He holds his schoolbag
very tight.
A boy alone.
Brave boy.
Surrounded.

FUCK OFF AND HAVE A GOOD HOLIDAY

Don't come back until you want to
and if you don't want to
don't come back.

DEEP

Slate grey waves
rising rushing
smacking hard
on crooked rock
hide me
for a while
hide me deep
hide me
hold me
clothe me
up and down
let me sleep
for a while
let me sleep
I am afraid.

MY TRAIN WAS MOVING SO SLOWLY THAT I WAS
ABLE TO WATCH THIS HAPPEN

The branches of the tree
with red berries on them
moved up with the wind
and down with the wind
and dipped the berries
into the deep waters
of a Highland loch.
When the berries
rose up out of the water
little drops fell down
and made splashes so tiny
that you could not hear them.
Then the branches dipped again.

I gazed down the railway carriage
and saw a man
who looked so like myself
in twenty years time
that he could only have been me.
I was dying to ask him
"How has it been?
Did you fall in love, laugh a lot,
find peace in your head,
regain the use of your arm
and conquer the world
with your poems?"
But he looked even crankier
than I do sometimes
so I just checked to see
if he was wearing
my hearing-aid.
. . . . Thanks be to God!
Twenty years on
and I still haven't lost it.

A NOTE WRITTEN TO VINCENT VAN GOGH ON A TRAIN BETWEEN CRIANLARICH AND OBAN

Dear Vincent
Today on the 28th of September 1995 at exactly 15.40
I understand perfectly why you cut your ear off.

The sea around the ferry
is hissing and thrashing
and fighting with the wash
spraying spit
spitting spray
waves crashing into waves
with white frenzy
and they are saying
come in come on
come on come in
and I am making
my knuckles white
standing there
looking down
into them.

Receive me with sweet suction
sweep me slowly in.
Isn't it warm.
Close in gently on me
from all sides
closer
close in
closer
till it is almost more
than you or I can bear.
Be still.
Now sweep me
further in.
I would like to stay like this
with you forever
or till one of us
or both of us together
gush out with the tide.

If my head explodes today it will be because
of all the happiness bursting around inside it.
Paddy is standing in Dunne's Stores doorway
throwing notes up into the wind from his banjo.
Little Anthony and Jimmy are sitting
with their backs against Madigan's wall
pretending to be hungry and homeless.
They will take £10 for their dog if they can get it.
Chrissie is shouting "LARGE TOBLERONES"
and when the winter sunlight strikes her pram
it angles away into silver.
Angela is pushing her empty pram
over to the market.
When she returns it will be heavy
with bananas and grapes.
The thousand tramp of feet is sharp
on hard brick.

BECAUSE DANNY IS THE REAL ONE AND THAT'S FOR SURE

Danny hadn't got the price of a cup of tea yesterday.
Now he is standing in front of me smoking a big cigar
and holding a plastic bag heavy with beer cans.
"I got a bit of work this morning . . . the church . . . John's Lane."
"Painting or what?"
"Not really . . . outside . . . beggin' . . . £45 . . . £45 in an hour.
This saint . . . eh . . . Rita . . . Saint Rita . . . her mass on a Saturday.
It's betther than the bingo . . . they come from all over . . .
Kildare an' everywhere."
"£45 . . . she's some saint."
"Some saint is right."
And off he went up the street.
Tangled hair.
Frizzledy beard.
Big cigar.
Bag full of cans.
Happy man.
Happy saint.

Paddy is standing in Dunnes Stores doorway
playing "Somewhere My Love" on his banjo.
The first time I heard that tune
I was locked behind a door
and they would not let me out.
When the nurse turned on the radio outside
it was "Somewhere My Love"
that came in underneath my door.
Paddy is standing in Dunnes Stores doorway
playing "Somewhere My Love" on his banjo.
I am standing outside the same pub
where once I drank a pint and a half
and later that night cut my arm open.
It is all coming together with the music.
I honestly believed that it was gone.

RICHER THAN CRUSHED GRASS

The traffic light suddenly embedded
a magnificent green emerald
in the wet road
left it there
for a few moments
then bled it to death.

The apples are far back when you look in
from the road.
You see them framed between the arms
of the hedge and the other trees.
You see them rich with red
                    rich with wet.
The children who loved to take them
are long gone now.
The man who chased them is long gone too.
In the garden
there is not a move anywhere.
The gate is rusted shut.

ACTION

If this was a film
a huge big concrete block
would fall from a great height
onto your boyfriend's head
and zap him into all eternity.
If this was a film
you would waken
with an urgent light in your eyes
and crash headfirst out
through your bedroom window
exclaiming – "I must surrender
myself utterly to an Irish poet
with a hearing aid, a limp
and a bald spot."
But it's not
so fuck it.

AND YOU CAN'T STOP

It is a fearful thing to waken suddenly in the night
and a wild noise is raging around inside you.
It makes you go so fast
that you lie there holding onto yourself.
It makes you go so fast
that your chest roars blue murder.
It makes you go so fast
that the bedroom walls can't stop you.
It is a fearful thing to waken suddenly in the night
and crash around between the four walls,
the ceiling and the floor.

BRITTLE

Her veins don't want to be in her hands anymore.
Her hands are shrinking and bulging them outwards.
Her head is shrinking too.
All the skin which was full
now gathers in drifts of wrinkles.
Her legs are bone and not much more.
It is difficult to stand up straight.
It is difficult to walk.
The smoke she sucks
from the cigarette stick
fills her up
and coughs her out.
It is hard.

ON A COLD OCTOBER DAY WHEN I STOOD IN THE STREET FOR 6 HOURS AND SOLD 2 BOOKS A FOREIGN GIRL MADE ME HAPPY

A broken cardboard box blew along the street and stopped at my feet.
I picked it up and wrote on it very carefully – "PLEASE BRING ME HOME AND LOVE ME. I AM AN ABANDONED BOX."
I waited until I saw someone who looked kind
and offered them the box to read.
The first three people shied away as if they were frightened.
A group of four girls took it and walked down the street
reading the words.
Then they threw it onto the ground.
One of them kicked it.
I picked it up and placed it beside a litter bin.
A little traveller boy stopped and stared at the words for a long time.
"What does it say?" he asked me.
I told him.
He grinned and walked away slowly
all the time turning and looking back
with a huge smile on his face.
I offered the box to a trio of young foreigners.
A girl took it and examined the words.
She pointed to "ABANDONED."
"What does this mean?"
"It means that nobody wants it."
Her eyes softened. She clasped the cardboard to herself.
"I take it" she said.
And she walked away holding the cardboard very gently.
I was happy.

I WAS DELIGHTED AT FIRST

When I woke this morning
I saw a green and brown Autumn leaf
resting on my pillow.
When I went downstairs
and made a cup of coffee
I noticed that the big oak tree outside
had fallen down
and utterly demolished my house.

DOWN THE LINE

The inner city kid on the small mountain bike
rode it straight at the traveller kid
and made him jump out of the way.
Then he wheeled around
and did it again.
For the first time today
he felt good about himself.

SPIT ON LADS LEST YOU DIE

You know the young Dublin hardmen
who walk with a cocky strut
and thrust their shoulders
and lunge their heads
and spit with such ferocity
that chips of concrete
fly up out of the pavement.
Well – An t-Ollamh Ephraim Karbeovah
has discovered during exhaustive tests
that unless these young men
spit once every ten paces
their hearts will stop.
So that's alright then.
Spit on lads.
Spit on with impunity.
We'd hate to lose you.

PLEASE STOP SAYING EVERYBODY CAN REMEMBER 'COS I CAN'T

If anybody can remember where I was
when President Kennedy was shot
will they please tell me
because I haven't got a clue.

BARE

Winter winds
left nothing
stripped the tree
black to the bark
ripped
the leaves asunder
thin stiff branches
thin bones
of the oldest man
you know
thin stiff branches
making shapes
between black fingers
making lace
against the sky.
Find the hidden birds.

WIRED

The speckles in his head
would drive you mad
by day
by night
they drive him
crazy
nighttime
fits and starts
that stop him
dead
doesn't know who
or what
this morning
when he dressed
he tied
himself
in knots
flicks and flecks
fire the lights
behind his eyes
connections
hiss and crack
big he is
and strong
big and strong
bewildered
lost a long time
gone
never coming
back
connections
hiss and crack
once he had
a name
now it's
all the same
fits and starts

that stop
him dead
speckles
in his head
they drive
him crazy.

Jesus – give him rest
or something like it.

DARK DECEMBER AFTERNOON

I stood for a very long time
outside Zerep's window
in Grafton Street
staring in at a pair of shoes
which were covered
with silver sparkles.
I moved my head slowly
from side to side
the sparkles came alive
with captured light.
Tiny pinpoints
sharp red
winked and sparked
pierced my eyes
with needle pricks
of bloody ice.
I stood for a time
speared by red.
I needed to bleed.
Then I walked on.

IN CASE SHE COMES

Women dump their men in doorways.
"Wait there – I'll only be a minute."
Women dump their men
all over town
abandoned men
obedient men
doing as they are told.
"Wait there – I'll only be a minute."
And they do
hour after hour
waiting
obediently waiting
thinking
murderously thinking
"What the hell is keeping you?
You said a minute.
Are you going to be all day?"
Murder
thinking murder
with blank faces
half the blazing day
abandoned
afraid to even stray
for just a minute
in case she comes
afraid to go away
for just a minute
in case she comes
love honour and obey
for just a minute
in case she comes.

Matthew Gilligan
was wee-weeing
on a train
and wondering
"In the history
of mankind
at any
given time
what is
the largest number
of men women ducks
geese rabbits mice
horses cows and so on
which ever
simultaneously
did a widdle."
And as he
deeply pondered
he pushed
the crucial plunger
and with
a powerful suck
and gurgle
it swept him
clean away.

A SILENCE LIKE NO OTHER
Handel's Messiah. The Chapel. St. Patrick's Training College,
Drumcondra, Dublin. 12th December 1995.
I was there because Kay invited me.

The choir suddenly stopped.
I shivered with the thrill of the silence.
The most exciting absence of sound
that I have ever known.
One hundred young voices
suspended over the edge of fulfilment.
Nothing more for two beats
of sweet anticipation.
Then the crash
      the power
      the thunder
of the final HALLELLUJAH!!!
God – it was great!

Today I stood outside Anne's Bakery and Restaurant
in North Earl Street six days before Christmas
and stared over at a second floor window
in the G.P.O.
directly into the eyeline of a man who stared out
during Easter Week 1916 at where I am now standing
with ice in his stomach and a rifle in his hands
and he saw that the night was quiet.
He had no way of knowing
if he would ever see the morning.
Whoever he was
I think of him today.

When the first shot was fired
all the birds flew away.

OH GOD NOT ANOTHER WEATHER POEM

A man who I have never seen before in my life
stopped beside me in the street this morning
and informed me
"It's not as cold as it was yesterday."

Quite truthfully I couldn't give a flying fuck
but I decided not to tell him that.
And I wouldn't have.
Then he further informed me
"Mind you it wasn't raining yesterday
although I suppose we can't have everything."

So I did.

I heard a sound in the kitchen
which I have never heard
anywhere in my house before.
It was a sound like hailstones
skittering against a corrugated
metal roof on a shed.
It was a sound like a porcupine
firing all its spines together
at point-blank range against
tightly stretched canvas.
It was a sound like a million
small boys with peashooters
peppering a sheet of thin plywood.
I turned around to witness Willow
with his tail erect spraying
a black plastic bag with jerky
passion and multiple fire-power.
Hail to thee blithe ginger tomcat.
No matter which way I mark my territory
I am not capable of producing an effect
which sounds like so many different things.
I hereby award thee the world's very first
INTERNATIONAL INDOOR SANDBLASTING
MEDAL IN PERPETUITY.
And a warehouse full of choicest Whiskas.

SEQUEL

A man with a blue helmet on his head
said to me today.

"You're absolutely right Pat – we don't"

"What?"

"Give a bollix."

"Oh."

Early this morning
as I was setting out my poems
a man gave me a cheery
Dublin greeting.

"Stick your books
up your arse Pat!"

It shall be done.

A QUESTION OF PRIORITIES

"I'm just going down to the jewellers
to buy me wife a locket.
If I've anything left
I'll come back to you."

OVERHEARD North Earl Street 14-12-95

"I'll kick your head in for ye ye little wanker ye!"

UP AND DOWN THE LADDER

When things were getting me down this Christmas
and I couldn't see much point to my life anymore
I used to stand outside Bonavox window in North Earl Street
and watch the poor mechanical Santa Claus
climbing up and down a red stepladder
until he was two rungs away from the top.
That was as far as he ever got
before jerking abruptly to a stop.
Then off he went into reverse
groaning with the weight of his sack
back back and back
cursing his way to the bottom.
Santy - I know exactly how you felt.
The same thing used to happen me
when I was playing Snakes and Ladders.
One long curvy bloody snake
just when I felt sure I was going to make it.
And everybody laughed.
Nobody told you but over in the G.P.O.
things were ten times worse.
One poor Godforsaken gnome was sawing
the same piece of wood since early December.
Oh Santy - I was tempted. I really was.
I was tempted to reach into your life
at dead of night with a glass cutters
and hoist you all the way to the top
and say "Ho Bloody Ho."
Then onwards wildly onwards
across the road to the G.P.O.
with a chainsaw
that gnomes and Santas might be free
but Santy mechanical Santy
who will do it for me?

A huge big block of very loud conversation
made a run for it when nobody was looking.
Out through an open window
of the Coffee Bar in The Writer's Museum
and away across the rooftops
frightening pigeons off their ledges
putting the heart across old ladies
wakening babies
terrorising tramps
filling empty soccer stadiums
sweeping in through letterboxes
shouting "We Know You!"
rushing down telephone lines
overcrowding answering machines
wreaking havoc in public libraries
hiding at the back in The National Theatre
roaring "Oh Yes It Is!" "Oh No It's Not!"
creeping up behind holy nuns
yelling "Show us your knickers!"
And when the fun was over
fading to a whisper
tiptoing into a nursery
hushing an infant to sleep.

GO IN AND HAVE A LOOK

The Cornish pasties
in Bewleys
of Westmoreland Street
look exactly like
little baby dinosaurs
with their necks
and tails chopped off.

I sincerely hope they're not.

I didn't see him coming. All of a sudden he was standing over me in the street with a long lost smile as if he wasn't sure what to expect from the world and the people in it so he wore this disturbed smile and hoped for the best.

"I'm manic depressive" he said as if that explained everything . . . the black underpants pulled up and out and overflowing his trousers . . . his body curved forward so that his head reached a place before the rest of him and you could shelter from the rain in under the overhang of him. Some of his clothes were too big and some of them were too small and his arms and legs weren't sure about where they fitted into anything.

"I'm manic depressive." He said it again and there was relief in his voice. I could see about thirty five or forty tired years in his body and only half that number in his face. "I've got a certificate. I can't work" he said and hauled it out crumpled and stained to show me. It made uneasy sense to him. It frightened me. He stood still for a very long time looking at the certificate and a longer time looking at me and his face seemed to be growing younger and younger and I wasn't his mother so he hurried very suddenly up the street crumpling his certificate and burying it in his deepest pocket.

Three weeks later he appeared again. Suddenly. Out of nowhere. His movements were clumsy inside a much too big yellow PVC lifeboat-man's coat and pull-up trousers. His news for me was urgent. The very first thing that he said. "I've found a cure for the manic depression. First I buy a pint of stout. When the barman isn't looking I put 15 sugars into it and slosh it all around. Then I drink it."

I told a woman what the man had said. All about the pint and the 15 sugars. "What a way to kill a pint" she said.

We're going to die anyway.

NO SUCH THING

The man sat in the coffee shop
and watched the open hatch
in the wall.
Cups, mugs, saucers and plates
moved slowly past on a conveyor belt.

"Hand me that shotgun"
he said to the waitress
and effortlessly blew six mugs
to smithereens.

"Congratulations" she said. "You
have just won a free dinner."

When he had eaten his prize
the waitress picked up the shotgun.

"Those six mugs come out of my wages
so hand over all your money."

"I will like hell" he replied. "I'll give you
the price of the mugs and that's it."

"No deal – your dinner comes out
of my wages as well."

"What sort of a coffee shop is this?"
he demanded.

"A very unfair one" she said
and she shot him.

YOU HAVE TO TELL SOMEONE

He waited until it was dark.
He turned his collar up and pulled his cap down.
He crept into the loneliest phone box that he could find
and dialled the Garda Confidential Number.

"Hello" he whispered.
"I wish to tell you something very secret."

"Go ahead."

"I eh . . . I . . . ."

"Go on."

"I've got piles and . . . and I scratch them
when nobody is looking."

"Did you rob them from someone?"

"God no . . . they came by themselves."

"That's alright then – Go in peace.
Your sins are forgiven."

And he danced a jig for joy.
Zippedydoo!
You would too.

OUT OF WATER

Kneeling forward on the timbers of the boatslip
bending over as near to the top of the water
as you can go.
The tide is high
the estuary as full as it dares
with flat green sea
making little sucking noises
under the timbers
and you looking down deep for crabs.
Not a move on the bottom
the seaweed keeping its secrets,
you watching for a little eruption
a murky cloud
an explosion of sand
but nothing moves.
All the time in the world
to kneel on timber
at one with the gulls
warm with the sun
safe with the sea
the smell of fish on your fingers,
soft bait tied on string
heavy with stone
and when you lower it
you make no sound
feeding it down
to rest near a world of weed.

How long you wait.

"Come out come out
wherever you are
come out
you excite me"
the thrill
the secret thrill of waiting.

A big one
green and dark
a big one
sideways slow scuttle
you looking down
the secret thrill
of looking down
a big one
clutching clawing
gripping my bait
take the strain
with very slow
and gentle weight
take the strain and test it
"Oh don't let go
hold on to my bait."
Slowly slowly up
with lazy fascination
green and dark creature
from the sea
holding on with one claw
sideways sliding up
following the ballet pull
of the string
inch over inch
towards the awful moment
when it swings above the water
and clings onto confusion.

I am thrilled.

A delight
to meet
you Jasmin !
With love,
from

For all street sellers
and street musicians
everywhere.
You are my heroes.

1/9/2006
DUBLIN

Other books by Pat Ingoldsby.

POETRY
You've Just Finished Reading This Title
Rhyme Doesn't With Reason
Up The Leg Of Your Jacket
Welcome To My Head (Please Remove Your Boots)
Salty Water
Scandal Sisters
How Was It For You Doctor?
Poems So Fresh And So New – Yahoo!

PROSE
The Peculiar Sensation Of Being Irish

FOR CHILDREN
Zany Tales
Tell Me A Story Pat (Tape)

Contents